WHAT GOT YOU HERE WON'T GET YOU THERE

Writers of the Round Table Press

Executive Editor
COREY MICHAEL BLAKE

Art Direction by
NATHAN BROWN

ROUND TABLE COMICS

WHAT GOT YOU HERE WON'T GET YOU THERE

MARSHALL GOLDSMITH
WITH MARK REITER

Adapted by
CULLEN
BUNN
AND
SHANE
CLESTER

Illustrated by
SHANE
CLESTER

© 2011 Writers of the Round Table Press
Round Table Comics

@RNDTABLECOMICS
WWW.ROUNDTABLECOMICS.COM

Round Table Companies
1670 Valencia Way
Mundelein, IL 60060
USA

Phone: 815-346-2398

First Edition: Oct 2011
ISBN: 978-1-61066-013-6

Printed in Canada

"As the CEO of the Girl Scouts, I was working to help a great organization be 'the best that we could be.' The first person Marshall volunteered to work with was me—this sent an important message. I was exuberant about the experience, I improved, and we moved this process across the organization. Twenty-four years later, I am the chairman of the Leader to Leader Institute—and we are still working together to serve leaders."
– Frances Hesselbein, winner of the Presidential Medal of Freedom

"We were a very successful team who took our performance to the next level. With Marshall's help we identified our two areas and went to work. We used everyone's help and support, exceeded our improvement expectations, and had fun! A team's dedication to continuous improvement combined with Marshall's proven improvement process ROCKS!"
– Alan Mulally, CEO, Ford Motor Company, former president and CEO, Boeing Commercial Airlines

"Marshall Goldsmith has helped me become a more effective leader, as judged by the people who are most important at Getty Images—our employees. Marshall has helped me and my executive team members to be much better positive role models for living our Leadership Principles."
– Jonathan Klein, CEO, Getty Images

"Marshall is a dynamo. He helps highly successful people get better and better and better. His advice helps me enormously at work, but it makes an even bigger impact at home. My wife and kids stand up and applaud Marshall for helping me become a better husband and dad. What could be better than that?"
– Mark Tercek, CEO, The Nature Conservancy, former managing director, Goldman Sachs & Co.

"At McKesson, we are on a mission—together with our customers—to fundamentally change the cost and quality of how heath care is delivered. To fully realize the potential that lies in this transformation, our leaders must be able to demonstrate values-based leadership practices to maximize employee engagement each and every day. Marshall's teachings remind us of how personal growth and change are a never-ending journey."
– John Hammergren, CEO, McKesson

ACKNOWLEDGEMENTS

What Got You Here Won't Get You There would not have been possible without the help and support of many people:

My wonderful clients who teach me every day more than I could ever teach them. As good as they are, they are still striving to get better!

My lovely wife, Lyda, son, Bryan, and daughter, Kelly, who help me keep everything in perspective and make life fun.

My collaborator and agent, Mark Reiter, who has helped me "find my voice" in print.

My friend and editor, Sarah McArthur, who endlessly reviews everything I write.

And, the wonderful folks at Round Table Companies, who came to me with this fun idea and have made the process so much fun!

Thank you!

INTRODUCTION

Few people are blessed with an internal compass that orients them automatically. You may have met one of these people once or twice in your life. Chances are one of them is your role model or hero. These people have an almost unerring sense of direction that guides them not only down the road, but also in their career, their marriage, and friendships. We admire these people. They know who they are, where they are going, and what they are doing.

Most of us do not go through life with this unerring sense of direction that never falters. Most of us have, somewhere along the way, lost our internal "You are here" compass. We don't know which way to go, which path to take, and we have no idea how our behavior comes across to our friends and family, clients, and customers. We have no idea that we are partaking in one, or more, of 20 very bad behavioral habits that are keeping us from being as successful as we really can be.

This little comic will show you simply what it looks like when:

- Someone thinks having all the answers is helpful, but it's really coming across as arrogance.
- Someone thinks she is contributing with helpful comments, but others feel it's really just butting in.
- Someone thinks he is holding his tongue, but the rest of the team sees it as being unresponsive.
- Someone thinks she is delegating effectively, but it really looks to everyone else as if she is shirking her responsibilities.

And so on it goes, until after time, these bad habits chip away at our families, teams, and organizations until we have a major crisis on our hands.

This little comic can be your map. It can help you to successfully make that career transition, work better with your team, and/or lead your organization. It can show you the way from here to there, and it can help you be successful. I hope you enjoy it as much as I do and that you share it with your friends, family, and co-workers. Enjoy the journey.

Life is good.
Marshall Goldsmith

YOU ARE HERE.

A FEW PEOPLE NEVER NEED MAPS.

SOME PEOPLE ACTUALLY GO THROUGH LIFE WITH THIS UNERRING SENSE OF DIRECTION.

IT GUIDES THEM IN THEIR SCHOOL YEARS, CAREERS, MARRIAGES, AND FRIENDSHIPS. THEY KNOW WHO THEY ARE AND WHERE THEY'RE GOING.

WE ALL KNOW PEOPLE LIKE THIS.

FOR SOME OF US, IT'S OUR MOMS OR DADS— PEOPLE WHO SERVED AS MORAL ANCHORS IN OUR STORMY CHILDHOODS.

FOR OTHERS, IT'S A COLLEGE PROFESSOR WHO WAS THE FIRST PERSON TO PUNCTURE OUR PRETENSIONS.

IT COULD EVEN BE A CELEBRITY.

WHAT ALL OF THESE ROLE MODELS HAVE IN COMMON IS AN EXQUISITE SENSE OF WHO THEY ARE, WHICH TRANSLATES INTO PERFECT PITCH ABOUT HOW THEY COME ACROSS TO OTHERS.

A FEW PEOPLE NEVER SEEM TO NEED ANY HELP IN GETTING TO WHERE THEY WANT TO GO. THEY HAVE A BUILT IN GPS MECHANISM.

THESE PEOPLE DO NOT NEED MY HELP.

MEETING ROOM

THE PEOPLE I MEET DURING THE COURSE OF MY WORKING DAY AS AN EXECUTIVE COACH ARE GREAT PEOPLE WHO MAY HAVE LOST THEIR INTERNAL "YOU ARE HERE" MAP.

AND THEY MAY BE PEOPLE WHO HAVE FALLEN INTO ANY ONE (OR MORE) OF THE TWENTY BAD HABITS OF SUCCESSFUL PEOPLE.

...SO THERE WE WERE, EASILY 100 THOUSAND LEAGUES UNDER THE SEA, JUST SWIMMING AND SWIMMING...

PEOPLE WHO ARE GUILTY OF ADDING TOO MUCH VALUE.

PEOPLE WHO ARE GUILTY OF PLAYING FAVORITES.

LT. HANDSOME, WOULD YOU LIKE TO DRIVE?

SURE!

OH, COME ON!

UH HUH! WHO'S YOUR DADDY??

WOOT! WOOT!

PEOPLE WHO ARE GUILTY OF WINNING TOO MUCH.

PEOPLE WHO ARE GUILTY OF AN EXCESSIVE NEED TO BE THEMSELVES.

THEY THINK THEY HAVE ALL THE ANSWERS, BUT OTHERS SEE IT AS ARROGANCE.

THEY THINK THEY'RE CONTRIBUTING TO A SITUATION, BUT OTHERS SEE IT AS BUTTING IN.

THEY THINK THEY'RE DELEGATING EFFECTIVELY, BUT OTHERS SEE IT AS SHIRKING RESPONSIBILITIES.

4

I WISH I HAD THE POWER TO SNAP MY FINGERS AND MAKE THESE PEOPLE IMMEDIATELY SEE THE NEED TO CHANGE.

BUT I CAN'T.

IT DOESN'T TAKE MUCH TO GET PEOPLE REORIENTED.

THE PROBLEMS WE'LL BE LOOKING AT ARE NOT LIFE-THREATENING DISEASES (ALTHOUGH IGNORED FOR TOO LONG THEY CAN DESTROY A CAREER).

...POINTING THEM OUT...

...SHOWING THE HAVOC THEY CAUSE AMONG THE PEOPLE SURROUNDING US, AND...

...DEMONSTRATING THAT WITH A SLIGHT BEHAVIORAL TWEAK WE CAN ACHIEVE A MUCH MORE APPEALING EFFECT.

THIS BOOK IS YOUR MAP—A MAP THAT CAN TURN A MAZE OF WRONG TURNS IN THE WORKPLACE INTO A STRAIGHT LINE TO THE TOP.

IN THE ARC OF A LONG CAREER, YOU WILL ALWAYS BE IN TRANSIT FROM "HERE" TO "THERE."

HERE CAN BE A GREAT PLACE. IF YOU'RE SUCCESSFUL, HERE IS EXACTLY THE KIND OF PLACE YOU WANT TO BE.

BUT HERE IS ALSO A PLACE WHERE YOU CAN BE A SUCCESS IN SPITE OF SOME GAPS IN YOUR BEHAVIOR OR PERSONAL MAKEUP.

YOU ARE HERE.

YOU CAN GET THERE.

BUT YOU HAVE TO UNDERSTAND THAT WHAT GOT YOU HERE WON'T GET YOU THERE.

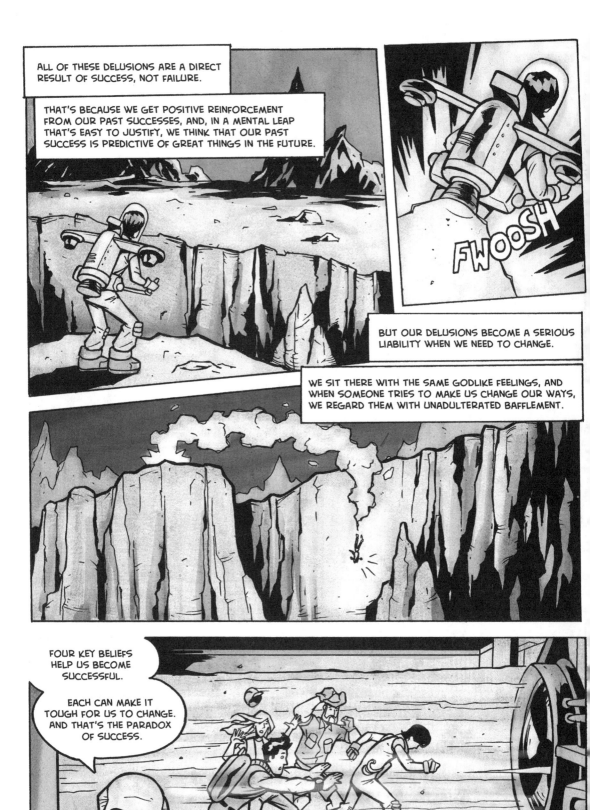

ALL OF THESE DELUSIONS ARE A DIRECT RESULT OF SUCCESS, NOT FAILURE.

THAT'S BECAUSE WE GET POSITIVE REINFORCEMENT FROM OUR PAST SUCCESSES, AND, IN A MENTAL LEAP THAT'S EASY TO JUSTIFY, WE THINK THAT OUR PAST SUCCESS IS PREDICTIVE OF GREAT THINGS IN THE FUTURE.

FWOOSH

BUT OUR DELUSIONS BECOME A SERIOUS LIABILITY WHEN WE NEED TO CHANGE.

WE SIT THERE WITH THE SAME GODLIKE FEELINGS, AND WHEN SOMEONE TRIES TO MAKE US CHANGE OUR WAYS, WE REGARD THEM WITH UNADULTERATED BAFFLEMENT.

FOUR KEY BELIEFS HELP US BECOME SUCCESSFUL.

EACH CAN MAKE IT TOUGH FOR US TO CHANGE. AND THAT'S THE PARADOX OF SUCCESS.

THESE BELIEFS THAT CARRIED US HERE MAY BE HOLDING US BACK IN OUR QUEST TO GO THERE.

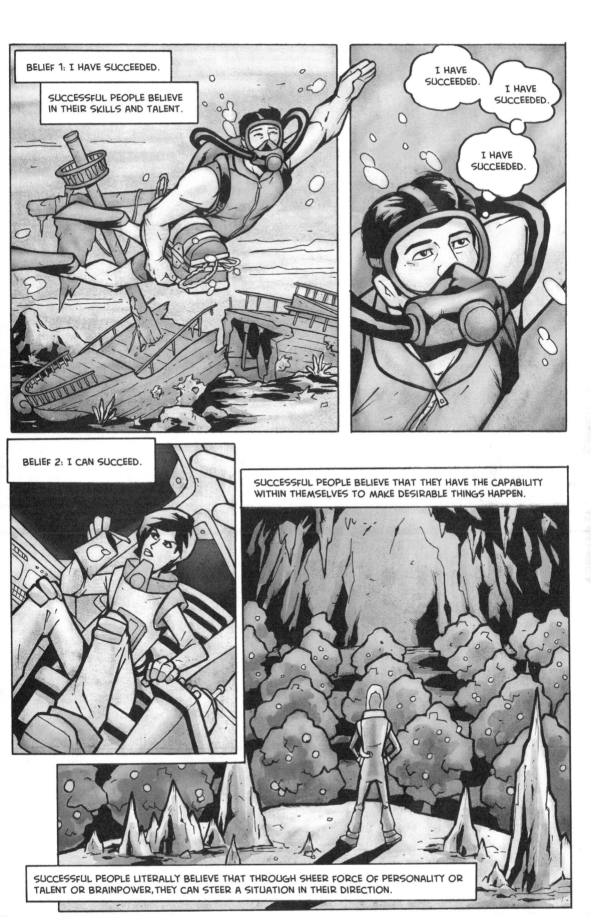

BELIEF 3: I WILL SUCCEED.

TODAY'S THE DAY.

THAT BIG LION'S OUT THERE AND WE'RE GOING TO GET HIM.

SUCCESSFUL PEOPLE HAVE AN UNFLAPPABLE OPTIMISM.

BELIEF 4: I CHOOSE TO SUCCEED.

SUCCESSFUL PEOPLE BELIEVE THAT THEY ARE DOING WHAT THEY DO, BECAUSE THEY CHOOSE TO DO IT.

WHEN WE DO WHAT WE HAVE TO DO, WE ARE COMPLIANT.

WHEN WE DO WHAT WE CHOOSE TO DO, WE ARE COMMITTED.

THESE FOUR SUCCESS BELIEFS MAKE US SUPERSTITIOUS.

MOST OF US SCORN SUPERSTITION AS SILLY BELIEFS OF THE PRIMITIVE AND UNEDUCATED.

DEEP DOWN INSIDE, WE ASSURE OURSELVES THAT WE'RE ABOVE THESE SILLY NOTIONS.

NOT SO FAST.

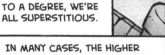

TO A DEGREE, WE'RE ALL SUPERSTITIOUS.

IN MANY CASES, THE HIGHER WE CLIMB THE ORGANIZATIONAL TOTEM POLE, THE MORE SUPERSTITIOUS WE BECOME.

PSYCHOLOGICALLY SPEAKING, SUPERSTITIOUS BEHAVIOR COMES FROM THE MISTAKEN BELIEF THAT A SPECIFIC ACTIVITY THAT IS FOLLOWED BY POSITIVE REINFORCEMENT IS ACTUALLY THE CAUSE OF THAT POSITIVE REINFORCEMENT.

PSYCHOLOGIST B.F. SKINNER WAS ONE OF THE FIRST TO HIGHLIGHT THIS INANITY BY SHOWING HOW HUNGRY PIGEONS WOULD REPEAT THEIR TWITCHES BECAUSE DOING SO WAS RANDOMLY FOLLOWED BY SMALL PELLETS OF GRAIN.

FROM MY EXPERIENCE, HUNGRY BUSINESSPEOPLE REPEAT CERTAIN BEHAVIOR ALL THE TIME, DAY IN AND DAY OUT, WHEN THEY BELIEVE LARGE PELLETS OF MONEY AND RECOGNITION WILL COME THEIR WAY BECAUSE OF IT.

ALMOST EVERYONE I MEET IS SUCCESSFUL BECAUSE OF DOING A LOT OF THINGS RIGHT...

AND ALMOST EVERYONE I MEET IS SUCCESSFUL IN SPITE OF SOME BEHAVIOR THAT DEFIES COMMON SENSE.

BEFORE WE CAN TALK ABOUT FIXING FAULTY BEHAVIOR, WE MUST IDENTIFY THE MOST COMMON FAULTS.

WHAT WE'RE DEALING WITH HERE ARE CHALLENGES IN INTERPERSONAL BEHAVIOR, OFTEN LEADERSHIP BEHAVIOR.

THEY ARE THE EGREGIOUS EVERYDAY ANNOYANCES THAT MAKE YOUR WORKPLACE SUBSTANTIALLY MORE NOXIOUS THAN IT NEEDS TO BE.

THEY ARE TRANSACTIONAL FLAWS BY ONE PERSON AGAINST ANOTHER.

THEY ARE...

WINNING TOO MUCH.

WOO HOO!

WE'RE ASTRONAUTS!!

ADDING TOO MUCH VALUE.

THIS IS THE TOOTH OF THE RARE BENGALI STRIPPED GATOR.

ONLY TWO IN THE WORLD, MATE.

PASSING JUDGMENT.

MAKING DESTRUCTIVE COMMENTS.

OH MY GOD! THAT IS THE UGLIEST THING I'VE EVER SEEN!

TELLING THE WORLD HOW SMART YOU ARE.

SPEAKING WHEN ANGRY.

WITHHOLDING INFORMATION.

NEGATIVITY.

FAILING TO GIVE PROPER RECOGNITION.

CLAIMING CREDIT THAT WE DON'T DESERVE.

MAKING EXCUSES.

IT'S NOT MY FAULT!

NOBODY TOLD ME THE PLANET WAS INHABITED!

PLAYING FAVORITES.

THAT'S A GOOD BOY! YES YOU ARE!

CLINGING TO THE PAST.

REFUSING TO EXPRESS REGRET.

I ABSOLUTELY MADE THE RIGHT CHOICE.

16

NOT LISTENING.

HELLO! I'M TALKING TO YOU!

THERE'S A BREACH IN THE HULL!

HUH?

FAILING TO EXPRESS GRATITUDE.

DON'T WORRY, I'VE STOPPED THE LEAK.

...

PUNISHING THE MESSENGER.

HOW DID THIS HAPPEN? WHY DIDN'T SOMEONE TELL ME?

PASSING THE BUCK.

GET SOME GUYS AND CLEAN THIS UP.

AN EXCESSIVE NEED TO BE "ME."

A LITTLE HELP?

MOPPING'S NOT REALLY "ME." I'M MORE OF A "SUPERVISOR."

WINNING TOO MUCH IS EASILY THE MOST COMMON BEHAVIORAL PROBLEM THAT I OBSERVE IN SUCCESSFUL PEOPLE.

HABIT #1: WINNING TOO MUCH.

LET'S BE CLEAR: I'M NOT DISPARAGING COMPETITIVENESS.

I'M POINTING OUT THAT IT'S A PROBLEM WHEN WE DEPLOY IT AT THE SERVICE OF OBJECTIVES THAT SIMPLY ARE NOT WORTH THE EFFORT.

WINNING TOO MUCH IS THE #1 CHALLENGE BECAUSE IT UNDERLIES NEARLY EVERY OTHER BEHAVIORAL PROBLEM.

OUR OBSESSION WITH WINNING REARS ITS NOISOME HEAD ACROSS THE SPECTRUM OF HUMAN ENDEAVOR, NOT JUST AMONG SENIOR EXECUTIVES.

WHEN THE ISSUE IS IMPORTANT, WE WANT TO WIN.

WHEN THE ISSUE IS TRIVIAL, NOT WORTH OUR TIME AND ENERGY, WE WANT TO WIN.

EVEN WHEN THE ISSUE IS CLEARLY TO OUR DISADVANTAGE, WE WANT TO WIN.

I WAS AT A BACKYARD PARTY ONCE WATCHING A ONE-ON-ONE BASKETBALL GAME BETWEEN A FATHER AND HIS 9-YEAR-OLD SON.

THE GAME STARTED OFF MERRILY AND NONCHALANTLY—WITH THE DAD GIVING THE YOUNG KID GIMMES AND DO-OVERS TO KEEP HIM ENTHUSED.

BUT ABOUT TEN MINUTES INTO THE ALLEGED FUN, THAT FATHER'S "GOTTA WIN" GENES KICKED IN, AND HE STARTED PLAYING AS IF THE SCORE MATTERED.

HE ACTUALLY TOOK PLEASURE IN BEATING HIS SON 11 BASKETS TO 2.

THAT'S HOW PERVASIVE THIS URGE TO WIN IS.

EVEN WHEN IT IS BEYOND TRIVIAL—WHEN IT CAN ACTUALLY SCAR SOMEONE WE LOVE—WE STILL WANT TO WIN.

IF THE NEED TO WIN IS THE DOMINANT GENE IN OUR DNA—THE OVERWHELMING REASON WE'RE SUCCESSFUL—THEN WINNING TOO MUCH IS A PERVERSE GENETIC MUTATION THAT CAN LIMIT OUR SUCCESS.

BOOYAH!

HA HA HA

WHAT I'M GOING TO SUGGEST REPEATEDLY IS THE HERETICAL NOTION THAT WE CAN BECOME MORE SUCCESSFUL IF WE APPRECIATE THIS "FLAW" AND WORK TO SUPPRESS IT IN OUR INTERPERSONAL RELATIONS.

HABIT #2: ADDING TOO MUCH VALUE.

IT IS EXTREMELY DIFFICULT FOR SUCCESSFUL PEOPLE TO LISTEN TO OTHER PEOPLE TELL THEM SOMETHING THAT THEY ALREADY KNOW WITHOUT COMMUNICATING SOMEHOW THAT (A) "WE ALREADY KNEW THAT" AND (B) "WE KNOW A BETTER WAY."

THAT'S THE PROBLEM WITH ADDING TOO MUCH VALUE.

IMAGINE YOU'RE THE CEO.

I COME TO YOU WITH AN IDEA THAT YOU THINK IS VERY GOOD.

IF WE DIVERT JUST 10% OF OUR RESOURCES FROM HYDROPONICS, WE'LL RUN 25% MORE EFFICIENTLY!

RATHER THAN JUST PAT ME ON THE BACK AND SAY, "GREAT IDEA!" YOUR INCLINATION (BECAUSE YOU HAVE VALUE TO ADD) IS TO SAY...

GOOD IDEA, BUT IT'D BE BETTER IF YOU TRIED IT THIS WAY.

LET'S DIVERT 25% FROM HYDROPONICS!

THE PROBLEM IS, YOU MAY HAVE IMPROVED THE CONCEPT OF MY IDEA BY 5 PERCENT, BUT YOU'VE REDUCED MY COMMITMENT TO EXECUTING IT BY 50 PERCENT, BECAUSE YOU'VE TAKEN AWAY MY OWNERSHIP OF THE IDEA.

MY IDEA IS NOW YOUR IDEA—
AND I WALK OUT OF YOUR
OFFICE LESS ENTHUSED ABOUT IT.

THAT'S THE FALLACY OF ADDING VALUE.

WHATEVER WE GAIN IN THE FORM OF
A BETTER IDEA IS LOST MANY TIMES
OVER IN OUR EMPLOYEES' DIMINISHED
COMMITMENT TO THE CONCEPT.

I'M NOT SAYING THAT BOSSES HAVE
TO ZIP THEIR LIPS TO KEEP THEIR
STAFF'S SPIRITS FROM SAGGING.

BUT THE HIGHER UP YOU GO IN THE ORGANIZATION, THE
MORE YOU NEED TO MAKE OTHER PEOPLE THE WINNERS
AND NOT MAKE IT ABOUT WINNING YOURSELF.

HABIT #3: PASSING JUDGMENT.

THERE'S NOTHING WRONG WITH OFFERING AN OPINION IN THE NORMAL GIVE AND TAKE OF BUSINESS DISCUSSIONS.

YOU WANT PEOPLE TO AGREE OR DISAGREE FREELY.

BUT IT'S NOT APPROPRIATE TO PASS JUDGMENT WHEN WE SPECIFICALLY ASK PEOPLE TO VOICE THEIR OPINIONS ABOUT US.

WHAT DO YOU THINK OF MY NEW SHARK CAGE DESIGN?

I DUNNO... I'D DO SOME MORE TESTING BEFORE TRYING IT OUT.

PEOPLE DON'T LIKE BEING CRITIQUED, HOWEVER OBLIQUELY. THAT'S WHY PASSING JUDGMENT IS ONE OF THE MORE INSIDIOUS WAYS WE PUSH PEOPLE AWAY AND HOLD OURSELVES BACK FROM GREATER SUCCESS.

WHAT ARE YOU? AN IDIOT? THIS DESIGN IS PERFECT!

THE ONLY SURE THING THAT COMES OUT OF PASSING JUDGMENT ON OTHER PEOPLE'S EFFORTS TO HELP IS THAT THEY WON'T HELP US AGAIN.

IF YOU WALK INTO THE EXAMINING ROOM WITH A BROKEN LEG, THE DOCTOR DOESN'T PASS JUDGMENT ON HOW YOU BROKE YOUR LEG.

HE DOESN'T CARE IF YOU BROKE YOUR LEG COMMITTING A CRIME OR KICKING A DOG OR TRIPPING DOWN THE STAIRS. HE ONLY CARES ABOUT FIXING YOUR LEG.

YOU NEED TO EXTEND THE SAME ATTITUDE— THE DOCTOR'S MISSION-NEUTRAL PURPOSE— TO DEALING WITH PEOPLE TRYING TO HELP YOU.

WHAT DO YOU THINK OF MY NEW SHARK CAGE DESIGN?

I DUNNO... I'D DO SOME MORE TESTING BEFORE TRYING IT OUT.

YOU ARE NOT ALLOWED TO JUDGE ANY HELPFUL COMMENT OFFERED BY A COLLEAGUE OR FRIEND OR FAMILY MEMBER.

NO MATTER WHAT YOU PRIVATELY THINK OF THE SUGGESTION, YOU MUST KEEP YOUR THOUGHTS TO YOURSELF, HEAR THE PERSON OUT, AND SAY...

THANK YOU.

FOR ONE WEEK TREAT EVERY IDEA THAT COMES YOUR WAY FROM ANOTHER PERSON WITH COMPLETE NEUTRALITY. THINK OF YOURSELF AS A HUMAN SWITZERLAND.

AFTER ONE WEEK, I GUARANTEE YOU WILL HAVE SIGNIFICANTLY REDUCED THE NUMBER OF POINTLESS ARGUMENTS YOU ENGAGE IN AT WORK OR AT HOME.

HABIT #4: MAKING DESTRUCTIVE COMMENTS.

THAT WASN'T A VERY BRIGHT DESIGN DECISION.

THIS IS NOT VERY WELL THOUGHT-OUT.

DO YOU REMEMBER THE TIME YOU FORGOT THE MATERIALS FOR THAT BIG JOB AND IT DELAYED US SEVERAL WEEKS?

DESTRUCTIVE COMMENTS ARE THE CUTTING SARCASTIC REMARKS WE SPEW OUT DAILY, WITH OR WITHOUT INTENTION, THAT SERVE NO OTHER PURPOSE THAN TO PUT PEOPLE DOWN, HURT THEM, OR ASSERT OURSELVES AS THEIR SUPERIORS.

$@#&*@!

ONCE THE COMMENT LEAVES YOUR LIPS, THE DAMAGE IS DONE AND IT'S VERY HARD TO UNDO.

CRASH

THEY ARE DIFFERENT FROM COMMENTS THAT ADD TOO MUCH VALUE—BECAUSE THEY ADD NOTHING BUT PAIN.

WE MAKE DESTRUCTIVE COMMENTS WITHOUT THINKING— AND THEREFORE WITHOUT NOTICING OR REMEMBERING. BUT THE OBJECTS OF OUR SCORN REMEMBER.

THERE, THERE..

SNIFF! SOB!

NO MATTER HOW FERVENTLY YOU APOLOGIZE—AND EVEN IF THE APOLOGY IS ACCEPTED—THE COMMENT LINGERS IN THE MEMORY.

SORRY.

THAT WASN'T A VERY BRIGHT DESIGN DECISION.

DESTRUCTIVE COMMENTS ARE AN EASY HABIT TO FALL INTO, ESPECIALLY AMONG PEOPLE WHO HABITUALLY RELY ON CANDOR AS AN EFFECTIVE MANAGEMENT TOOL.

TROUBLE IS... CANDOR CAN EASILY BECOME A WEAPON. PEOPLE PERMIT THEMSELVES TO ISSUE DESTRUCTIVE COMMENTS UNDER THE EXCUSE THAT THEY ARE TRUE.

THE FACT THAT A DESTRUCTIVE COMMENT IS TRUE IS IRRELEVANT. THE QUESTION IS NOT, "IS IT TRUE?" BUT RATHER...

IS IT WORTH IT?

BEFORE SPEAKING, ASK YOURSELF:

WILL THIS COMMENT HELP OUR CUSTOMERS?

WILL THIS COMMENT HELP OUR COMPANY?

WILL THIS COMMENT HELP THE PERSON I'M TALKING TO?

WILL THIS COMMENT HELP THE PERSON I'M TALKING ABOUT?

IF THE ANSWER IS NO, THE CORRECT STRATEGY DOES NOT REQUIRE A PH.D.

DON'T SAY IT.

HABIT #5: STARTING WITH "NO," "BUT," OR "HOWEVER."

WHEN YOU START A SENTENCE WITH "NO," "BUT," "HOWEVER," OR ANY VARIATION THEREOF, NO MATTER HOW FRIENDLY YOUR TONE OR HOW MANY CUTE MOLLIFYING PHRASES YOU THROW IN TO ACKNOWLEDGE THE OTHER PERSON'S FEELINGS, THE MESSAGE TO THE OTHER PERSON IS BLUNTLY AND UNEQUIVOCALLY...

WHAT YOU'RE SAYING IS WRONG, AND WHAT I'M SAYING IS RIGHT.

NOTHING PRODUCTIVE CAN HAPPEN AFTER THAT.

TOLD YOU...

FOR ONE WEEK MONITOR YOUR COWORKERS' USE OF "NO," "BUT," AND "HOWEVER."

KEEP A SCORECARD OF HOW MANY TIMES EACH INDIVIDUAL USES THOSE WORDS AT THE START OF A SENTENCE.

AT THE VERY LEAST, YOU'LL BE SHOCKED AT HOW COMMONLY USED THESE WORDS ARE.

STOP TRYING TO DEFEND YOUR POSITION AND START MONITORING HOW MANY TIMES YOU BEGIN REMARKS WITH "NO," "BUT," OR "HOWEVER."

HABIT #6: TELLING THE WORLD HOW SMART WE ARE.

WE NEED TO WIN PEOPLE'S ADMIRATION.

WE NEED TO LET THEM KNOW THAT WE ARE AT LEAST THEIR INTELLECTUAL EQUAL IF NOT THEIR SUPERIOR. WE NEED TO BE THE SMARTEST PERSON IN THE ROOM.

AND THAT'S WHEN I DISCOVERED THIS DEEP SEA CREATURE... SOMETHING NEVER ENCOUNTERED BEFORE!

IT USUALLY BACKFIRES.

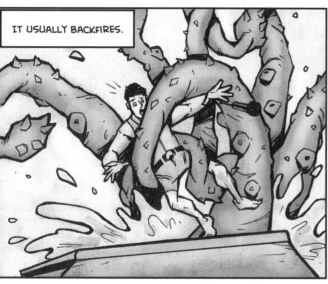

HAVE YOU EVER DONE THIS?

YOUR ASSISTANT DASHES INTO YOUR OFFICE WITH A DOCUMENT THAT NEEDS YOUR IMMEDIATE ATTENTION.

SIR... I THINK THIS CREATURE MAY BE DANGEROUS...

WHAT YOUR ASSISTANT DOESN'T KNOW IS THAT YOU'VE ALREADY BEEN ALERTED TO THE SITUATION A FEW MINUTES EARLIER.

DO YOU ACCEPT THE DOCUMENT AND THANK YOUR ASSISTANT? OR DO YOU FIND SOME WAY TO MAKE YOUR ASSISTANT AWARE THAT YOU ARE PRIVY TO THE INFORMATION?

THE IMPLICATION IS THAT YOUR ASSISTANT HAS JUST WASTED YOUR TIME.

PAUSE BEFORE OPENING YOUR MOUTH TO ASK YOURSELF, "IS ANYTHING I SAY WORTH IT?"

CONCLUDE THAT IT ISN'T.

AND SAY, "THANK YOU."

HABIT #7: SPEAKING WHEN ANGRY.

ANGER HAS ITS VALUE AS A MANAGEMENT TOOL, I GUESS. BUT AT WHAT PRICE?

SO THIS IS ALL THE INVADER HAD ON HIM?

EMOTIONAL VOLATILITY IS NOT THE MOST RELIABLE LEADERSHIP TOOL.

I WOULDN'T OPEN THAT.

WHEN YOU GET ANGRY, YOU ARE USUALLY OUT OF CONTROL. IT'S HARD TO LEAD PEOPLE WHEN YOU'VE LOST CONTROL.

I'M THE CAPTAIN!

I'LL DO WHAT I WANT!

?

KOFF! KOFF! KOFF!

URK!

IT'S VERY HARD TO PREDICT HOW PEOPLE WILL REACT TO ANGER.

THEY WILL SHUT DOWN AS OFTEN AS THEY PERK UP.

RAAARRR!!

BUT THE WORST THING ABOUT ANGER IS HOW IT STIFLES OUR ABILITY TO CHANGE.

ONCE YOU GET A REPUTATION FOR EMOTIONAL VOLATILITY, YOU ARE BRANDED FOR LIFE. PRETTY SOON THAT IS ALL PEOPLE KNOW ABOUT YOU.

A LEGEND TELLS OF A YOUNG FARMER WHO WAS COVERED WITH SWEAT AS HE PADDLED HIS BOAT UP THE RIVER. HE WAS GOING UPSTREAM TO DELIVER HIS PRODUCE.

AS HE LOOKED AHEAD, HE SPIED ANOTHER VESSEL, HEADING RAPIDLY DOWNSTREAM TOWARD HIS BOAT.

CHANGE DIRECTION, YOU IDIOT! YOU ARE GOING TO HIT ME!

THE OTHER VESSEL HIT HIS BOAT WITH A SICKENING THUD.

THUD!

YOU MORON!

HOW COULD YOU MANAGE TO HIT MY BOAT IN THE MIDDLE OF THIS WIDE RIVER?

AS HE LOOKED AT THE OTHER VESSEL, HE REALIZED THAT THERE WAS NO ONE IN THE OTHER BOAT.

THE LESSON IS SIMPLE.

THERE IS NEVER ANYONE IN THE OTHER BOAT. WHEN WE ARE ANGRY, WE ARE SCREAMING AT AN EMPTY VESSEL.

I CAN HELP YOU LOSE YOUR REPUTATION AS A PERSON WHO GETS ANGRY WITH ONE SIMPLE PIECE OF ADVICE.

I WOULDN'T OPEN THAT.

IF YOU KEEP YOUR MOUTH SHUT, NO ONE CAN KNOW HOW YOU REALLY FEEL. YOU HAVE TO SUPPRESS YOUR NATURAL INCLINATION AND BITE YOUR TONGUE.

BUT ONCE YOU APPRECIATE THE PAYOFF OF SAYING NOTHING— THAT IF YOU'RE SILENT, YOU CANNOT MAKE AN ASS OF YOUR- SELF OR MAKE AN ENEMY OUT OF SOMEONE ELSE—

THEN YOU MIGHT HAVE A CHANCE OF GETTING BETTER.

MAYBE I'LL HAVE IT EXAMINED FIRST.

HABIT #8: NEGATIVITY, OR "LET ME EXPLAIN WHY THAT WON'T WORK."

THIS DOCTOR HAS STRONG HERB.

IT'S THE CURE YOU'VE BEEN SEARCH- ING FOR.

WE ALL KNOW NEGATIVE PEOPLE—PEOPLE WHO ARE CONSTITUTIONALLY INCAPABLE OF SAYING SOMETHING POSITIVE OR COMPLIMENTARY TO ANY OF YOUR SUGGESTIONS.

YOU COULD WALK INTO THE OFFICE WITH THE CURE FOR CANCER AND THE FIRST WORDS OUT OF THEIR MOUTHS WOULD BE...

LET ME EXPLAIN WHY THAT WON'T WORK.

"LET ME EXPLAIN WHY THAT WON'T WORK" IS UNIQUE BECAUSE IT IS PURE, UNADULTERATED NEGATIVITY UNDER THE GUISE OF BEING HELPFUL.

IF NEGATIVITY IS YOUR FLAW, MY FIRST IMPULSE WOULD BE TO HAVE YOU MONITOR YOUR STATEMENTS THE MOMENT SOMEONE OFFERS YOU A HELPFUL SUGGESTION.

IF YOU CATCH YOURSELF FREQUENTLY SAYING, "LET ME TELL YOU WHY THAT WON'T WORK," YOU KNOW WHAT NEEDS FIXING.

THE MORE REVEALING CLUE WOULD BE TO TAKE A PERSONAL INVENTORY OF HOW YOUR COLLEAGUES DEAL WITH YOU.

HOW OFTEN DO THEY COME TO YOU WITH HELPFUL SUGGESTIONS—WITHOUT HAVING TO ASK? HOW OFTEN DO THEY KNOCK ON YOUR DOOR AND SIT DOWN TO SHOOT THE BREEZE OR GIVE YOU A HEADS-UP ABOUT A DEVELOPMENT THAT MIGHT AFFECT YOU?

HABIT #9: WITHHOLDING INFORMATION.

INTENTIONALLY WITHHOLDING INFORMATION IS THE OPPOSITE OF ADDING VALUE. WE ARE DELETING VALUE. YET IT HAS THE SAME PURPOSE: TO GAIN POWER.

YOU SEE IT IN PEOPLE WHO EXAGGERATE THE VIRTUE OF KEEPING A SECRET; THEY USE IT AS AN EXCUSE TO LEAVE YOU OUT OF THE INFORMATION FLOW.

YOU SEE THE PEOPLE WHO ANSWER EVERY QUESTION WITH A QUESTION; THEY BELIEVE REVEALING ANYTHING PUTS THEM AT A DISADVANTAGE.

YOU SEE IT IN ITS PASSIVE-AGGRESSIVE INCARNATION IN PEOPLE WHO DON'T RETURN YOUR PHONE CALLS OR ANSWER YOUR E-MAILS OR ONLY GIVE PARTIAL ANSWERS TO YOUR QUERIES.

COME IN... COME IN... HAVE YOU FOUND THE LEAK IN THE PIPELINE?

REFLECT ON HOW YOU FELT ABOUT THE FOLLOWING EVENTS:

A MEETING YOU WEREN'T TOLD ABOUT.

HEY, YOU HAVE TO DISCONNECT YOUR POWER CABLE FROM THE SHIP.

HUH?

A MEMO OR E-MAIL YOU WEREN'T COPIED ON.

URK!

DIDN'T YOU GET THE MEMO?

A MOMENT WHEN YOU WERE THE LAST PERSON TO LEARN SOMETHING.

THE PROBLEM WITH NOT SHARING INFORMATION IS THAT IT RARELY ACHIEVES THE DESIRED EFFECT.

YOU MAY THINK YOU'RE GAINING AN EDGE AND CONSOLIDATING POWER, BUT YOU'RE ACTUALLY BREEDING MISTRUST. IN ORDER TO HAVE POWER, YOU NEED TO INSPIRE LOYALTY RATHER THAN FEAR AND SUSPICION.

WHAT I'M DESCRIBING HERE IS NOT JUST THE WILLFUL REFUSAL TO SHARE INFORMATION.

I PREFER TO FOCUS ON ALL THE UNINTENTIONAL OR ACCIDENTAL WAYS WE WITHHOLD INFORMATION.

35

WE DO THIS WHEN WE'RE TOO BUSY TO GET BACK TO SOMEONE WITH VALUABLE INFORMATION.

WE DO THIS WHEN WE FORGET TO INCLUDE SOMEONE IN OUR DISCUSSIONS OR MEETINGS.

WHAT IS THIS THING?

NOT NOW! KINDA BUSY!

AIM FOR THE RESPIRATOR!

WHERE'S THAT?

WE DO THIS WHEN WE DELEGATE THE TASK TO OUR SUBORDINATES BUT DON'T TAKE THE TIME TO SHOW THEM EXACTLY HOW WE WANT THE TASK DONE.

HOW DO YOU STOP WITHHOLDING INFORMATION?

SIMPLE ANSWER: START SHARING IT.

THE BASE OF IT'S HELMET!!

YOU SEE IT?

GOT IT!

ZAP

HABIT #10: FAILING TO GIVE PROPER RECOGNITION.

IN WITHHOLDING YOUR RECOGNITION OF ANOTHER PERSON'S CONTRIBUTION TO A TEAM'S SUCCESS, YOU ARE NOT ONLY SOWING INJUSTICE AND TREATING PEOPLE UNFAIRLY BUT YOU ARE DEPRIVING PEOPLE OF THE EMOTIONAL PAYOFF THAT COMES WITH SUCCESS.

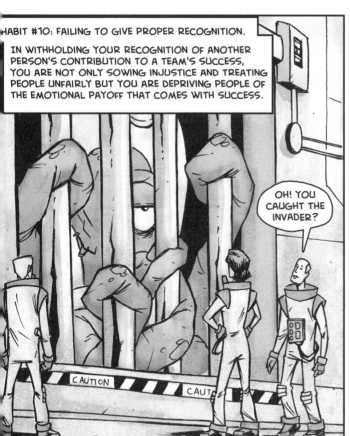

OH! YOU CAUGHT THE INVADER?

THEY CANNOT REVEL IN THE SUCCESS WORKS OF CONGRATULATIONS-- BECAUSE YOU HAVE CHOKED OFF THAT OPTION.

YEAH! YOU SHOULD HAVE SEEN IT!

INSTEAD THEY FEEL FORGOTTEN, IGNORED, PUSHED TO THE SIDE. AND THEY RESENT YOU FOR IT.

RECOGNITION IS ALL ABOUT CLOSURE. IT'S THE BEAUTIFUL RIBBON WRAPPED AROUND THE JEWEL BOX THAT CONTAINS THE PRECIOUS GIFT OF SUCCESS YOU AND YOUR TEAM HAVE CREATED.

WHEN YOU FAIL TO PROVIDE RECOGNITION, YOU ARE CHEAPENING THE GIFT.

ONE OF MY CLIENTS TAUGHT ME A WONDERFUL TECHNIQUE FOR IMPROVING IN THE AREA OF PROVIDING RECOGNITION.

HE MADE A LIST OF ALL THE IMPORTANT GROUPS OF PEOPLE IN HIS LIFE. HE THEN WROTE DOWN THE NAMES OF EVERY IMPORTANT PERSON IN EACH GROUP.

DID SOMEONE DO SOMETHING THAT I SHOULD RECOGNIZE?

IF THE ANSWER WAS "YES" HE GAVE THEM SOME VERY QUICK RECOGNITION.

CAPTAIN ROGERS HERE TOOK THE SHOT. GREAT AIM, BUDDY!

HA HA! THANKS!

HABIT #11: CLAIMING CREDIT THAT WE DON'T DESERVE.

CLAIMING CREDIT IS ADDING INSULT TO THE INJURY THAT COMES WITH OVERLOOKED RECOGNITION.

HEY! UP HERE! TAKE MY HAND!

THE BEST WAY TO STOP BEING A CREDIT HOG IS TO DO THE OPPOSITE.

WHEN SOMEONE YOU WORK WITH STEALS THE CREDIT FOR A SUCCESS THAT YOU CREATED, THEY'RE COMMITTING THE MOST RAGE-INDUCING INTERPERSONAL "CRIME" IN THE WORKPLACE.

SHARE THE WEALTH. HERE'S A SIMPLE DRILL THAT WILL TRANSFORM YOU FROM A CREDIT MISER TO A CREDIT PHILANTHROPIST.

FOR ONE DAY MAKE A MENTAL NOTE OF EVERY TIME YOU PRIVATELY CONGRATULATE YOURSELF ON AN ACHIEVEMENT, LARGE OR SMALL.

IF YOU'RE LIKE ME, YOU'LL FIND THAT YOU PAT YOURSELF ON THE BACK MORE OFTEN THAN YOU THINK DURING A NORMAL DAY.

WOW! ARE YOU GUYS OK? THAT WAS AMAZING!

ONCE YOU'VE ASSEMBLED THE LIST, TAKE APART EACH EPISODE AND ASK YOURSELF IF IT'S IN ANY WAY POSSIBLE THAT SOMEONE ELSE MIGHT DESERVE THE CREDIT FOR "YOUR" ACHIEVEMENT.

PRETTY QUICK THINKING ON MY PART, HUH?

IF ANY OF THE OTHER PEOPLE INVOLVED IN YOUR EPISODES WERE LOOKING AT THIS SITUATION, WOULD THEY ACCORD YOU AS MUCH CREDIT AS YOU ARE CLAIMING FOR YOURSELF?

HABIT #12: MAKING EXCUSES.

THERE SIMPLY IS NO EXCUSE FOR MAKING EXCUSES. WHEN YOU HEAR YOURSELF SAYING "I'M SORRY I'M LATE BUT THE TRAFFIC WAS MURDER." STOP TALKING AT THE WORD "SORRY."

BLAMING THE TRAFFIC IS A LAME EXCUSE—AND DOESN'T EXCUSE THE FACT THAT YOU KEPT THE OTHER PEOPLE WAITING.

I LIKE TO DIVIDE EXCUSES INTO TWO CATEGORIES: BLUNT AND SUBTLE.

THE BLUNT "DOG ATE MY HOMEWORK" EXCUSE SOUNDS LIKE THIS:

I'M SORRY I MISSED OUR LUNCH DATE. MY ASSISTANT HAD IT MARKED DOWN FOR THE WRONG DAY ON MY CALENDAR.

THE PROBLEM WITH THIS TYPE OF EXCUSE IS THAT WE RARELY GET AWAY WITH IT.

UH HUH... I MADE THE APPOINTMENT WITH YOU, NOT YOUR ASSISTANT.

THE MORE SUBTLE EXCUSES APPEAR WHEN WE ATTRIBUTE OUR FAILINGS TO SOME INHERITED DNA THAT IS PERMANENTLY LODGED WITHIN US.

I'M IMPATIENT.

I ALWAYS PUT THINGS OFF TO THE LAST MINUTE.

I'VE ALWAYS HAD A QUICK TEMPER.

IT'S AMAZING HOW OFTEN I HEAR OTHERWISE BRILLIANT, SUCCESSFUL PEOPLE MAKE WILLFULLY SELF-DEPRECATING COMMENTS ABOUT THEMSELVES.

THE NEXT TIME YOU HEAR YOURSELF SAYING, "I'M JUST NO GOOD AT ..." ASK YOURSELF, "WHY NOT?"

HABIT #13: CLINGING TO THE PAST.

THERE IS A SCHOOL OF THOUGHT AMONG PSYCHOLOGISTS AND BEHAVIORAL CONSULTANTS THAT WE CAN UNDERSTAND A LOT ABOUT OUR ERA BEHAVIOR BY DELVING INTO THE PAST.

THIS SCHOOL BELIEVES, "WHEN IT'S HYSTERICAL, IT'S HISTORICAL."

IF YOU'RE A PERFECTIONIST OR CONSTANT APPROVAL SEEKER, IT'S BECAUSE YOUR PARENTS NEVER SAID YOU WERE GOOD ENOUGH. IF YOU OPERATE ABOVE THE RULES AND FEEL YOU CAN DO NO WRONG, IT'S BECAUSE YOUR PARENTS DOTED ON YOU AND INFLATED YOUR IMPORTANCE.

THAT SCHOOL IS ON PERMANENT RECESS HERE.

GOING BACKWARDS IS NOT ABOUT CREATING CHANGE. IT'S ABOUT UNDERSTANDING.

???

WHO ARE YOU? WHAT DO YOU WANT?

I'M YOU! FROM THE FUTURE!

THERE'S NOTHING WRONG WITH UNDERSTANDING. UNDERSTANDING THE PAST IS PERFECTLY ADMISSIBLE IF YOUR ISSUE IS ACCEPTING THE PAST.

YOU HAVE TO GO WITH ME.

BUT IF YOUR ISSUE IS CHANGING THE FUTURE, UNDERSTANDING WILL NOT TAKE YOU THERE.

WHERE?

TO THE FUTURE!!

HABIT #14: PLAYING FAVORITES.

I HAVE REVIEWED CUSTOM-DESIGNED LEADERSHIP PROFILES OF MORE THAN 100 MAJOR CORPORATIONS.

THESE DOCUMENTS TYPICALLY FEATURE BOILERPLATE LANGUAGE THAT DESCRIBES THE LEADERSHIP BEHAVIOR EACH COMPANY DESIRES.

NOT ONE PROFILE HAS EVER INCLUDED THE DESIRED BEHAVIOR THAT READ "EFFECTIVELY SUCKS UP TO MANAGEMENT." GIVEN THE DEDICATION TO FAWNING AND SUCKING UP IN MOST CORPORATIONS— AND HOW OFTEN SUCH BEHAVIOR IS REWARDED— IT PROBABLY SHOULD.

LEADERS CAN STOP ENCOURAGING THIS BEHAVIOR BY FIRST ADMITTING THAT WE ALL HAVE A TENDENCY TO FAVOR THOSE WHO FAVOR OF US, EVEN IF WE DON'T MEAN TO.

WE SHOULD THEN RANK OUR DIRECT REPORTS IN THREE CATEGORIES.

YEAH!! WHOO-HOO!!

ALL RIGHT!!

HOW MUCH DO THEY LIKE ME?

WHAT IS THEIR CONTRIBUTION TO THE COMPANY AND ITS CUSTOMERS? ARE THEY A PLAYERS, B, C, OR WORSE?

HOW MUCH POSITIVE PERSONAL RECOGNITION DO I GIVE THEM?

IF WE ARE HONEST WITH OURSELVES, OUR RECOGNITION OF PEOPLE MAY BE LINKED TO HOW MUCH THEY SEEM TO LIKE US RATHER THAN HOW WELL THEY PERFORM.

THAT'S THE DEFINITION OF PLAYING FAVORITES.

HABIT #15: REFUSING TO EXPRESS REGRET.

EXPRESSING REGRET, OR APOLOGIZING, IS A CLEANSING RITUAL

YOU SAY, "I'M SORRY"— AND YOU FEEL BETTER.

BUT LIKE MANY THINGS THAT ARE FINE IN THEORY, IT'S HARD FOR MANY OF US TO DO.

REFUSING TO APOLOGIZE CAUSES AS MUCH ILL WILL IN THE WORKPLACE (AND AT HOME) AS ANY OTHER INTERPERSONAL FLAW.

APOLOGIZING IS ONE OF THE MOST POWERFUL AND RESONANT GESTURES IN THE HUMAN ARSENAL.

THE BEST THING ABOUT APOLOGIZING IS THAT IT FORCES EVERYONE TO LET GO OF THE PAST.

I CAN'T CHANGE THE PAST. ALL I CAN SAY IS I'M SORRY FOR WHAT I DID WRONG. I'M SORRY IT HURT YOU. THERE'S NO EXCUSE FOR IT AND I WILL TRY TO DO BETTER IN THE FUTURE.

I WOULD LIKE YOU TO GIVE ME ANY IDEAS ABOUT HOW I CAN IMPROVE.

THAT STATEMENT—AN ADMISSION OF GUILT, AN APOLOGY, AND A PLEA FOR HELP—IS TOUGH FOR EVEN THE MOST COLD-HEARTED AMONG US TO RESIST.

HABIT #16: NOT LISTENING.

PEOPLE WILL TOLERATE ALL SORTS OF RUDENESS, BUT THE INABILITY TO PAY ATTENTION HOLDS A SPECIAL PLACE IN THEIR HEARTS—PERHAPS BECAUSE IT'S SOMETHING ALL OF US SHOULD BE ABLE TO DO WITH EASE.

WHEN YOU FAIL AT LISTENING YOU'RE SENDING OUT AN ARMADA OF NEGATIVE MESSAGES.

I DON'T CARE ABOUT YOU.

I DON'T UNDERSTAND YOU.

YOU'RE WASTING MY TIME.

YOU'RE WRONG.

THE INTERESTING THING ABOUT NOT LISTENING IS THAT, FOR THE MOST PART, IT'S A SILENT, INVISIBLE ACTIVITY. PEOPLE RARELY NOTICE YOU DOING IT.

THE ONLY TIME PEOPLE ACTUALLY SEE THAT YOU'RE NOT LISTENING TO THEM IS WHEN YOU'RE DISPLAYING EXTREME IMPATIENCE.

WHEN YOU FIND YOURSELF MENTALLY OR LITERALLY DRUMMING YOUR FINGERS WHILE SOMEONE ELSE IS TALKING, STOP THE DRUMMING.

STOP DEMONSTRATING IMPATIENCE WHEN LISTENING TO SOMEONE.

HABIT #17: FAILING TO EXPRESS GRATITUDE.

TO ME, THE TWO SWEETEST WORDS IN THE LANGUAGE ARE "THANK YOU."

IT WILL NEVER ANNOY THE PERSON HEARING IT.

GRATITUDE IS A SKILL THAT WE COULD NEVER DISPLAY TOO OFTEN, AND YET FOR SOME REASON, WE ARE CHEAP AND CHARY WITH GRATITUDE.

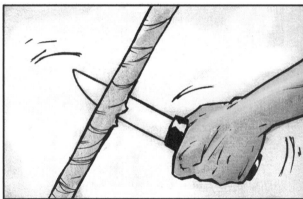

THEY'RE NOT ONLY DISARMING AND PLEASANT TO THE EAR, BUT THEY HELP US AVOID MANY PROBLEMS. LIKE APOLOGIZING, THANKING IS A MAGICAL SUPER-GESTURE OF INTERPERSONAL RELATIONS.

OF ALL THE BEHAVIORAL CHALLENGES WE'RE COVERING HERE, THIS ONE SHOULD BE THE EASIEST TO CONQUER.

PICK SOMETHING TO BE GRATEFUL FOR. SAY, "THANK YOU." DO IT NOW.

THANKS!

HABIT #18: PUNISHING THE MESSENGER.

PUNISHING THE MESSENGER MANIFESTS ITSELF IN BIG AND LITTLE WAYS.

IT'S NOT MERELY THE UNJUST RETALIATORY ACTION WE TAKE AGAINST A WHISTLEBLOWER OR THE ANGRY TIRADE WE KEEP UPON AN EMPLOYEE WHO TELLS US SOMETHING WE DON'T ENJOY HEARING.

THOSE SUPPLIES YOU ORDERED ARE RUNNING LATE.

IT'S ALSO THE SMALL RESPONSES WE MAKE THROUGHOUT THE DAY WHENEVER WE ARE INCONVENIENCED OR DISAPPOINTED.

@#$!%#!

IF YOUR GOAL WAS TO STOP PEOPLE FROM GIVING YOU INPUT—OF ALL KINDS—PERFECT YOUR REPUTATION FOR SHOOTING THE MESSENGER.

ALL YOU NEED TO SAY IS...

THANK YOU.

HABIT #19: PASSING THE BUCK.

TAKE A HEALTHY DOSE OF NEEDING TO WIN AND MAKING EXCUSES.

MIX IT WITH REFUSING TO APOLOGIZE AND FAILING TO GIVE PROPER RECOGNITION.

SPRINKLE IN A FAINT HINT OF PUNISH THE MESSENGER AND GETTING ANGRY.

AND WHAT YOU END UP WITH IS PASSING THE BUCK. BLAMING OTHERS FOR OUR MISTAKES.

WHAT'S STRANGE ABOUT PASSING THE BUCK IS THAT UNLIKE THE OTHER FLAWS LISTED HERE, WHICH WE ARE RARELY AWARE OF, WE DON'T NEED OTHER PEOPLE TO POINT OUT THAT WE'RE PASSING THE BUCK.

WE'RE WELL AWARE OF IT. WE KNOW WE MUST SHOULDER THE BLAME FOR FAILURE, BUT WE CAN'T BRING OURSELVES TO DO IT.

SO WE FIND A SCAPEGOAT.

INFALLIBILITY IS A MYTH. NO ONE EXPECTS US TO BE RIGHT ALL THE TIME.

IF PASSING THE BUCK IS YOUR CHALLENGE, YOU'RE PROBABLY ALREADY AWARE THAT YOU'RE DOING IT.

MY GOAL HERE IS TO MAKE YOU SEE THAT YOU'RE NOT FOOLING ANYONE—EXCEPT PERHAPS YOURSELF—AND THAT NO MATTER HOW MUCH YOU THINK YOU'RE SAVING YOUR HIDE, YOU'RE ACTUALLY KILLING IT.

HABIT #20: AN EXCESSIVE NEED TO BE "ME."

EACH OF US HAS A PILE OF BEHAVIOR WHICH WE DEFINE AS "ME."

IT'S THE CHRONIC BEHAVIOR, BOTH POSITIVE AND NEGATIVE, THAT WE THINK OF AS OUR INALTERABLE ESSENCE.

IF WE ARE IMPORTABLE PROCRASTINATORS WHO HABITUALLY RUIN OTHER PEOPLE'S TIMETABLES, WE DO SO BECAUSE WE'RE BEING TRUE TO "ME."

IF WE ALWAYS EXPRESS OUR OPINION, NO MATTER HOW HURTFUL OR NONCONTRIBUTORY IT MAY BE, WE ARE EXERCISING OUR RIGHT TO BE "ME."

THIS EXCESSIVE NEED TO BE "ME" IS ONE OF THE TOUGHEST OBSTACLES TO MAKING POSITIVE LONG-TERM CHANGE IN OUR BEHAVIOR.

KEEP THIS IN MIND WHEN YOU FIND YOURSELF RESISTING CHANGE BECAUSE YOU'RE CLINGING TO A FALSE—OR POINTLESS— NOTION OF "ME."

IT'S NOT ABOUT YOU. IT'S ABOUT WHAT OTHER PEOPLE THINK OF YOU.

TAKE A BREATH. TAKE A DEEPER BREATH.

NO ONE CAN DEFINE 'THERE' FOR YOU. IF SOME PEOPLE THINK YOUR VISION OF A WELL-LIVED LIFE IS A BIT GOOFY OR OFFBEAT, WHO CARES? IT ISN'T THEIR LIFE. IT'S YOURS.

FEW OF US WILL ACHIEVE ALL OF OUR DREAMS. SOME DREAMS WILL ALWAYS ELUDE US.

SO THE QUESTION IS NOT, "DID I MAKE ALL MY DREAMS COME TRUE?"

THE KEY QUESTION IS, "DID I TRY?"

ARE YOU FINDING MEANING AND HAPPINESS NOW? IS YOUR WORK EXCITING AND DO YOU LOVE WHAT YOU'RE DOING?

DO YOU LIKE THE PEOPLE? ARE THEY YOUR FRIENDS? DOES IT FEEL LIKE A TEAM OR A FAMILY?

CAN YOU FOLLOW YOUR DREAMS? IS THE ORGANIZATION GIVING YOU A CHANCE TO DO WHAT YOU REALLY WANT TO DO IN LIFE?

KNOW THAT YOU NEED TO BE HAPPY NOW, TO ENJOY YOUR FRIENDS AND FAMILY, TO FOLLOW YOUR DREAMS.

"A great coach teaches you how to improve yourself. Marshall is a great coach! He has a unique ability to help you determine what you can improve and what will have the greatest impact on the people you lead and love."
– Brian Walker, CEO, Herman Miller

"In his charming, rascal-like manner, Marshall is able to address uncomfortable issues in a non-threatening way. As a result, not only does the leader get better—the whole team gets better!"
– George Borst, CEO, Toyota Financial Services

"Marshall has helped me personally to improve as a leader and has provided the tools and dynamics to turn a well functioning management team into a high-performance team where all the members have improved individually and considerably added to team performance."
– David Pyott, CEO, Allergan

"While Cessna focused on continuous improvement of business results, Marshall helped me focus on leadership team continuous improvement. The impact is amazing. His practical no-nonsense approach is making a positive impact both professionally and personally on all of us. I have never had so much fun working on such a tough topic. Thank you, Marshall!"
– Jack Pelton, CEO, Cessna

"Marshall Goldsmith is the world's greatest coach because he has extraordinary life skills, the ability to connect deeply with others while remaining objective, and a passion for sharing everything he knows. He focuses—and helps others to focus—on what matters most in life, and brings unforgettable insights and excitement to every encounter."
– Sally Helgesen, global expert on developing women leaders and author of *The Female Vision*, **the** *Female Advantage,* **and** *The Web of Inclusion*

ABOUT MARSHALL GOLDSMITH

Dr. Marshall Goldsmith has recently been recognized as one of the 15 most influential business thinkers in the world, in a global bi-annual study sponsored by *The (London) Times*. Other acknowledgments include: *American Management Association* – top 50 thinkers and leaders who have influenced the field of management over the past 80 years, *Institute for Management Studies* – lifetime achievement award (one of two ever awarded), *Wall Street Journal* – top 10 executive educators, *Forbes* – 5 most-respected executive coaches, Economic Times (India) – top CEO coaches of America and *Fast Company* – America's preeminent executive coach. Marshall is one of a select few executive advisors who have been asked to work with over 120 major CEOs and their management teams. He is the million-selling author of numerous books, including *New York Times* best-sellers, MOJO and *What Got You Here Won't Get You There* – a Wall Street Journal #1 business book and winner of the Harold Longman Award for business book of the year.

ABOUT SHANE CLESTER

At six years old, Shane Clester realized that most people aren't happy with their jobs. Even as he drew robots just to see if he could, he decided at that young age that he would turn his artistic play into work. As Shane grew older and studied the nuances of art, his initial excitement evolved into fascination. He was compelled by the replication of life through seemingly limited tools, and embarked on a quest to learn technical proficiency.

In the early 2000s, Shane studied briefly under Jim Garrison, well-known for his art anatomy and technical skills. Shane then relocated from Arizona to California, where he learned a powerful lesson: You have to study to be an artist, and then you have to learn the business of being an artist.

Shane discovered that he needed to sell himself before he could sell a product. Over the course of the next several years, he broadened his portfolio to include youth-oriented art and comic books, and sourced clients by attending conferences and book fairs. Some of his clients have included leading comic book publisher IDW, Hasbro, Scholastic, Macmillan, and Times of London. Of his many projects, Shane is particularly proud of *Skate Farm: Volume 2*, a graphic novel he produced, *Mi Barrio*, a comic book adaptation of Robert Renteria's *From the Barrio to the Board Room,* and *The Prince* by Niccolò Machiavelli.

Please visit **www.MarshallGoldsmithLibrary.com** and check out all of my articles, audios and videos. You may download, copy and share this material in any way that you wish. So far, visitors from 195 countries have read, watched or listened to resource materials over 6.4 million times.

Life is good.
Marshall

The book that inspired the comic...

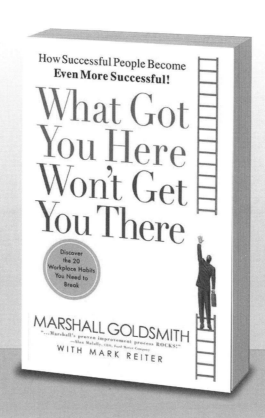

Available everywhere books are sold.

COMING SOON FROM ROUND TABLE COMICS

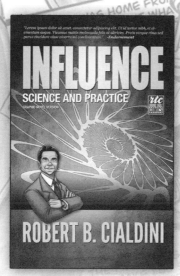
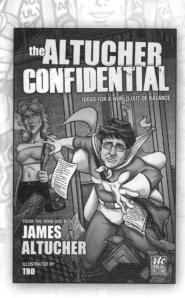

For more information visit:
www.roundtablecompanies.com

Follow us:
@RndTableCompanies